IMAGES OF SCOTLAND

EDINBURGH
OLD TOWN

IMAGES OF SCOTLAND

EDINBURGH
OLD TOWN

SUSAN VARGA

The
History
Press

Frontispiece: Cowgate by Peter Smeaton Rennie, 1905.

First published in 2006 by Tempus Publishing
Reprinted 2007

Reprinted in 2009 by
The History Press
The Mill, Brimscombe Port,
Stroud, Gloucestershire, GL5 2QG
www.thehistorypress.co.uk

Reprinted 2012

British Library Cataloguing in Publication Data.
A catalogue record for this book is available from the British Library.

ISBN 978 0 7524 4083 5

Typesetting and origination by Tempus Publishing Limited.
Printed and bound in Great Britain by
Marston Book Services Limited, Didcot

Contents

Acknowledgements

Thanks to Fiona Myles and my colleagues in the Edinburgh Room for their help and support with compiling this book; to Peter Stubbs, photographer and web-author of www.edinphoto. org.uk for being a wonderful source of information; to Wendy French, the best friend ever, for laborious proof reading; to my mother and father for endless babysitting to allow me to work on this project and to my long suffering husband, James, who has put up with piles of paper everywhere and a distinct lack of housework.

My gratitude to the following photographers and families who kindly gave me their permission to use photographs in this book – James L.A. Evatt; the *Evening News*; Barbara Hill; Dr Frank Rushbrook CBE and other members of the Rushbrook family; Trevor Yerbury.

A huge amount of thanks goes to the Edinburgh Photographic Society (EPS) who allowed me to use forty of their photographs in this compilation. The EPS was formed in 1861 and has been supporting both professional and amateur photographers ever since. From their beautiful premises at Great King Street in Edinburgh's New Town they provide darkroom, studio and library facilities and have weekly lectures on photography. They have the most wonderful collection of photography and regularly display work both on their website at www.edinburghphotographicsociety.co.uk and at exhibitions. Immense thanks to Anne Rogers and the EPS Committee for all their help.

Every effort has been made to locate copyright holders and seek permission for the use of all photographs in this book. If we have missed anyone then we apologise here.

Introduction

...this old black city, which was for all the world like a rabbit-warren, not only by the number of its indwellers, but the complication of its passages and holes.

Robert Louis Stevenson

Edinburgh is a city divided – into the old and the new. The medieval Old Town lies along the crag and tail of an extinct volcano and towers menacingly above the surrounding landscape. From the eighteenth century it faced its counterpart the impressive Georgian New Town over the drained valley of the Nor' Loch. Unlike many cities that found their character expunged with the encroachment of every new century's style, Edinburgh has retained the essence of its medieval heart and clung on to its roots. This book is a celebration of the nucleus from which this wonderful city has grown and developed into one of the most outstanding cultural centres in the world.

Edinburgh, the capital of Scotland, embodies much of what exemplifies the Scots – our fierce attachment to our past and culture; our intelligent, inventive, scientific and medical minds; our joy in congregation and celebration. More and more however we find that Edinburgh belongs to the world not just to the Scottish people. Hardly a month goes by without a cultural festival taking over Edinburgh's streets and venues; it is home to the Edinburgh International Festival and Fringe, the Military Tattoo, the International Book, Film, Science, Television Festivals and others too numerous to mention. Edinburgh opens its arms to the world and asks it to come and celebrate everything that makes life worth living.

With its amazing and unique architecture Edinburgh has been designated a UNESCO World Heritage Site, thus identifying it as having world importance in terms of its cultural and natural heritage. Recently too the city has received the accolade of becoming the first UNESCO City of Literature due to its and Scotland's literary culture. Edinburgh is perhaps as much built on books as it is on rock with its centres of learning, libraries, literary societies, publishing history and authors who have captured the imagination of the world. I don't believe it is a coincidence that the city has bred such creativity, it is a city that inspires.

Edimbourg, ville de l'Archeveche de St Andre a present siege episcopale Protestant (Edinburgh, town of the archdiocese of St Andrew, under siege by Episcopalian Protestants) by Pierre Aveline, *c.* 1650. View of Edinburgh at the time of Cromwell's siege, in retaliation for the Scot's proclamation of Charles II, following the execution of Charles I.

The Old Town of Edinburgh originated from an Iron Age fort, which by medieval times developed into a walled city almost surrounded by a thirty foot high wall. The wall added to the naturally defensive position of the town and contained seven gates that opened and shut at dawn and dusk allowing the city to control who entered for the purposes of security and levying taxes. The images in this book cover the area that is today known as the Royal Mile – stretching from the royal residences of Edinburgh Castle to the Palace of Holyroodhouse, the road is indeed one mile, and 106 yards. Historically though this relatively short span was greatly divided, most importantly into two separate burghs – that of Edinburgh and the Canongate. Within the Burgh of Edinburgh the Royal Mile was also split into the streets of Castlehill, the Lawnmarket and the High Street, each having a unique purpose and character. As well as those sections that make up the Royal Mile images have been included of areas attached to the main spine. These include the ancient Grassmarket and the George IV Bridge that thrust out from the ancient roadway and signalled the end of the Old Town's dominance of Edinburgh's history and locality. Although many of these pictures detail what has been lost, there is much that remains today.

The images in this book all come from the collections of the Edinburgh Room, Central Library on George IV Bridge. The Edinburgh Room has the most comprehensive collection in the world of material relating to Edinburgh. A core part of their collection is illustrative and presents a pictorial history of the city in prints, photographs, paintings, maps, drawings and slides. The contents of this book represent a tiny proportion of the 60,000 illustrations held by the Edinburgh Room, which cover all facets of the city's geography, history and culture. If you have any enquiries relating to any of the images in this book please contact: edinburgh.room@edinburgh.gov.uk or telephone 0131 242 8060.

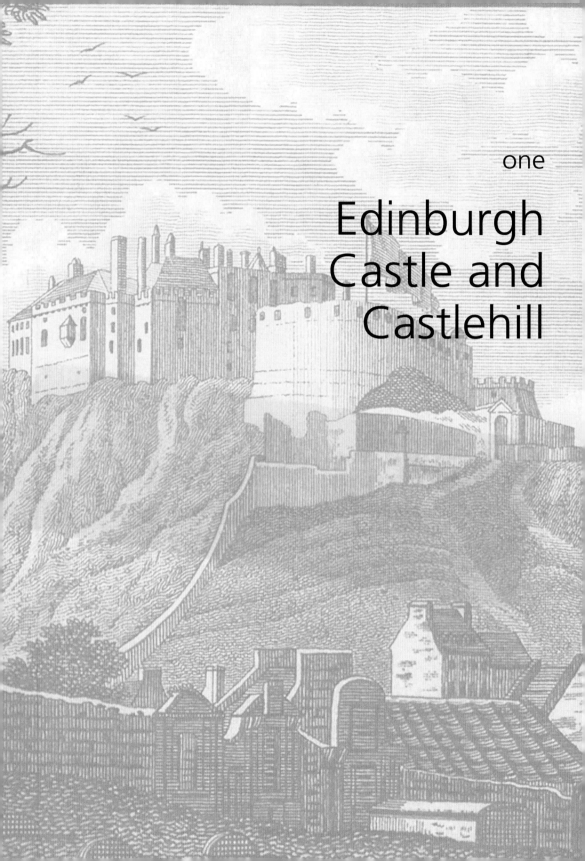

one

Edinburgh Castle and Castlehill

The Castle Rock is the reason for the very existence of Edinburgh. A basalt volcanic plug rising 437 feet above sea level, it provides the perfect impregnable defensive position. Surrounded by steep cliffs on all but the east side and the Nor' Loch to the north, it towered above the surrounding landscape. It is believed that habitation first began here around 900 BC with a settlement of Bronze Age round houses. By the sixth century the Votadini or Gododdin tribe had built a fort on the rock known as Din Eidyn (Fort of Eidyn) but in 638 it was wrested from them by the Angles from Yorkshire. The site once again fell into Scottish hands in 1018 when King Malcolm II defeated the English and secured the lands north of the River Tweed. A castle was soon built on the rock, beginning the castle's history as a royal residence.

Over the next ten centuries the castle has been extended and rebuilt many times by successive kings. All that remains of the ancient fortress is St Margaret's Chapel which was built around 1110 by King David as a memorial for his mother Queen Margaret, who was later canonised. Following Mary Queen of Scots marriage to the Earl of Bothwell and the revolt that it caused amongst the Scots nobility (leading to her flight to England) the castle was under siege for a year. It was held by supporters of the Queen in 1572 but was virtually reduced to rubble by the canons sent by Queen Elizabeth. It was rebuilt after the 'Lang Siege' and much of what can be seen now dates from this period of rebuilding. As most of the reconstruction concentrated on defences rather than royal apartments, the monarchy's residence in Edinburgh switched to Holyroodhouse. The castle still serves as an Army headquarters today but it is also managed by Historic Scotland and is the country's top tourist visitor attraction.

The entrance to Edinburgh Castle is via the castle esplanade; this wide flat parade ground links the fortifications to the area known as Castlehill. This was the first residential area to spring up outside the castle and naturally formed as close to the defences as possible for protection. There is nothing left of the original buildings as these were constructed of wood and little evidence of the successive mansions that were constructed here in the seventeenth century.

Edinburgh Castle from Greyfriars churchyard by Moses Griffith, *c.* 1780. Griffith was a Welsh artist but travelled around the country doing work for travel books and commissions from landowners.

Right: Edinburgh Castle from the Grassmarket by Thomas Begbie, *c.* 1857. The rounded section of the castle on the right-hand side is the half-moon battery. It was built in the late sixteenth century to give a wide angle of protection to the canons firing from behind it.

Below: South-east view of Edinburgh Castle from the Cowgate, *c.* 1930. Taken from buildings on George IV Bridge, this view shows the Cowgate leading into the Grassmarket. The tower on the far right is the edge of the Magdalen Chapel. Even from this height the Castle towers over the scene.

Opposite above: Castle Bank by Walter Geikie, *c.* 1830. Castle Bank was the area now inhabited by Johnston Terrace and here the artist has captured a snapshot of Edinburgh life. Geikie was born in Edinburgh in 1795 and became deaf due to a childhood illness. He went on to become a very successful artist specialising in scenes of lower class life often with a quirky humorous touch.

Left: Edinburgh Castle from the Grassmarket by John T. Knight, 1947. A very atmospheric view of the Castle with the smoke from numerous chimneys and the typically stormy Edinburgh sky. This view is taken from Cowgatehead at the foot of Candlemaker Row.

Below: Edinburgh Castle from King Stables Road, *c.* 1850. The English built a stable here in the fourteenth century to service the palace on the Castle Rock and the area had assumed the name King Stables by 1578.

CASTLE FROM KING'S STABLES. 20.

Edinburgh Castle from Greyfriar's churchyard by George Malcolm, *c.* 1940. The plume of smoke is a sure sign that the one o'clock gun has just gone off at the castle. The gun has been fired at Edinburgh since 1861 and was originally a way of letting ships in Leith Harbour reset their clocks to an accurate time.

Left: Johnston Terrace by Alexander A. Inglis, *c.* 1900. The palace on the left-hand side of the castle was the official home of the Stewart monarchy. James VI was born here and it was completely remodelled for his homecoming from London in 1617.

Below: Castle Terrace showing the old armoury, *c.* 1896. The long barracks building was built between 1796–99 to house the soldiers fighting in the war with the French. It created space for a 600–strong infantry battalion.

Edinburgh Castle from Princes Street Gardens by William Reid, 1930. A view across a snowy Princes Street Gardens towards Mills Mount on the Castle from where the one o'clock gun is fired.

Castle from the Vennel by Archibald Burns, *c*. 1868. The Vennel runs down to the Grassmarket along the edge of the Flodden and Telfer city walls. It was a very popular spot for artists to paint the castle from.

Scottish National War Memorial by George Malcolm, *c.* 1940. Stands in Crown Square on the very top of the Castle Rock, it was built to commemorate the 150,000 Scottish casualties of the First World War and went on to be a memorial for the Second World War and all subsequent campaigns. It was designed in 1927 by Sir Robert Lorimer and created by 200 Scottish artists and craftsmen.

Mons Meg by Alexander A. Inglis, 1900. Mons Meg is a bombard or siege gun that was gifted to James II in 1457 by his uncle Philip, Duke of Burgundy. The canon could fire missiles a distance of two miles but the barrel burst in 1681 and it has never been fired since.

Part of Edinburgh Castle near Argyle Tower and the 92nd Gordon Highlanders by David Octavius Hill and Robert Adamson, April 1846. Preparing to fire? The Gordon Highlanders pose beside a canon at the Forewall Battery. They are being watched from the gallery above by fellow soldiers and wives.

Castle esplanade with the Camerons leaving for the Front, 1914. The Cameron Highlanders leaving Edinburgh Castle during the First World War watched by crowds of family and friends. Edinburgh Castle is the site for the Scottish National War Memorial which contains books of the names of the dead from the war and a memorial to the fallen Cameron Highlanders.

Castle esplanade, 1907. The esplanade was created as a parade ground in 1753 by filling in the ridge between the castle and Castle Hill with rubble taken from the demolished buildings of the Royal Exchange site on the High Street. During the eighteenth century it was customary for the well-to-do citizens of Edinburgh to undertake a promenade on the esplanade.

Castle Wynd South by G.T. Kennedy,
1957.

Castle Wynd North from Johnston
Terrace by Thomas Begbie, c. 1860.
Castle Wynd originally led down to
the Grassmarket until the building of
Johnston Terrace in the 1830s which
cut straight across it. To the right
of the Wynd is the Gordon House,
home of the Duke of Gordon.

Left: Front of the Gordon House from Johnston Terrace by Alexander A. Inglis, 1900. The Gordon House was demolished in the nineteenth century and replaced by Castlehill School. This was the home of George, Duke of Gordon in the 1680s, defender of Edinburgh Castle against Bonnie Dundee in 1689.

Below: Houses removed for the building of Castlehill, *c.* 1860. The settlement at Castlehill pre–dates the rest of the burgh. The first settlement obviously grew up close to the protection of the castle, it was however separated from the fortifications by a deep trough in the rock.

Somerville's Land on Castlehill by Dr Thomas Keith, *c.* 1855. Somerville's Land was a timber and stone tenement, built in around 1580 and named after Bartholomew Somerville, a wealthy merchant. He donated a large amount of money to Edinburgh University in 1640, allowing for the foundation of the chair of divinity. The building was demolished in the 1880s.

Castlehill by Alexander A. Inglis, 1887. This view of Castlehill includes the entrance to Brown's Close and an assortment of shops including Leonard Small, collar maker, a commercial lodging and a general smallware shop.

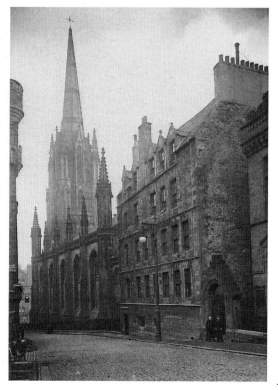

Castlehill, Edinburgh Photographic Society, 1870. The spire of the Victoria Hall, the Assembly Hall for the Church of Scotland towers above the other buildings of Castlehill. It was built between 1842-45 and partially designed by Augustus Welby Pugin who also worked on the Houses of Parliament. After the union of the Church of Scotland and the United Free Church the building was used as a church by various congregations until the early 1980s. It was renamed the Highland Tolbooth St John's church in the 1950s.

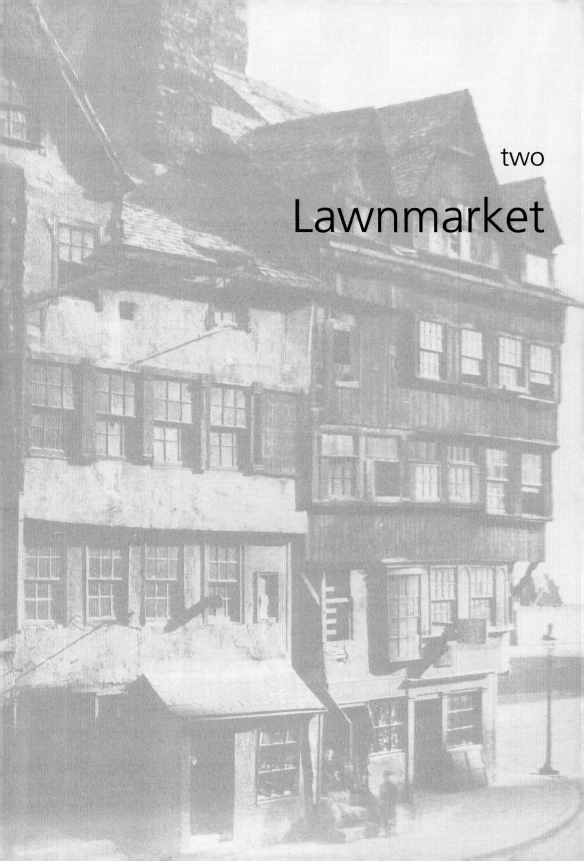

two
Lawnmarket

The Lawnmarket lies between Castlehill and the High Street and is 510 feet long. Apart from the Grassmarket it was the only other area of open space in the Old Town. In 1477 James III reorganised the markets of the burgh and established a cloth market here. Tables were placed down the middle of the street which were piled high with bales of material for sale. The market continued up until the nineteenth century. The name Lawnmarket probably comes from a corruption of the term 'Landmercat' which was where the goods brought in from outside the burgh were sold. 'Lawn' however is also a word for light cotton or linen and may relate to the cloth market.

In the eighteenth century the Lawnmarket was a very fashionable area of Edinburgh and a place of residence for the wealthy, particularly due to its closeness to Parliament House. It was the site of building developments such as Milne's Court which was built as housing for some of the richest families in Edinburgh. It offered what more traditional closes and lands (a tall narrow tenement) couldn't – light and space round an open courtyard. It is also home to the historically important Gladstone's Land and Lady Stair's House.

Above: Bowhead House by Dr Thomas Keith, 1856. Thomas Keith was a surgeon and amateur photographer who took photographs of Edinburgh and Iona in the 1850s. His images of architecture and landscape were mostly captured in the early morning as he felt that the light was more favourable then. He seems to have ceased his interest in photography in 1857 to concentrate on his medical career.

Opposite: Corner of the Lawnmarket and the West Bow by Thomas Begbie, 1857. Here a horse and cart is travelling up the steep slope of Johnston Terrace towards the triangular roof of the Bowhead House. This road was built twenty years previously as a 'New Western Approach' to the entry through the Grassmarket.

Above: Studding at Johnston Terrace by George Malcolm, *c.* 1930. Metal studs being driven into the road down the middle of Johnston Terrace. This was no doubt in response to the growing number of cars on the streets of Edinburgh, necessitating the need to have definite sides of the road for travelling on.

Opposite below: Corner of the West Bow, *c.* 1870. Bowhead House on the corner of the West Bow was a sixteenth-century timber-clad burger's house. The projecting front was supported by beams creating an arcade at ground level under which merchants sold their wares. By 1878 the building was in a poor state and was demolished only to be rebuilt six years later.

Right: 'To satisfy thirsty souls' by Richard Grant, 1954. Beer being delivered to one of the many taverns that have always been a feature of the Lawnmarket and High Street. Edinburgh was the original melting pot with people from all strata of society meeting in the taverns, from vagabonds to lawyers, literary men to merchants.

Below: Brodies Close, south side of the Lawnmarket, *c.* 1900. This close was named after the wright (builder), Francis Brodie, who ran a business from the Lawnmarket with his son, the notorious William (Deacon) Brodie. Respectable businessman by day and thief by night, William Brodie was hanged in 1788 on the gallows he had himself designed.

Left: Gladstone's Land before restoration by Francis M. Chrystal, *c.* 1912. Built in 1550 and acquired by the merchant and burgess Thomas Gledstanes, this was a classic Edinburgh 'land' or tenement. It had six storeys all of which apart from the ground and first floor were accessed from the turnpike stair at the front of the building. At ground level there were open stalls for merchants to sell their wares.

Below: Fish sellers by George Malcolm, *c.* 1930. Women wrapped up against the biting Edinburgh wind whilst selling fish on the Lawnmarket.

Right: Corner of Bank Street and the Lawnmarket by Francis M. Chrystal, 1912. Bank Street was created in 1798 to give access to the Mound which was being created as a way of reaching the developing New Town.

Below: North side of the Lawnmarket, *c.* 1875. In the middle of this row of tenements is the tall thin Gladstone's Land near the entry to Lady Stairs Close. The close gives access to Lady Stairs House which dates from 1622 and now houses the Writers Museum.

Left: South side of the Lawnmarket by Edinburgh Photographic Society, *c.* 1900. Libberton's Wynd was on the south side of the Lawnmarket, roughly where George IV Bridge is (at the left-hand side of the photograph). It was the site of the execution of William Burke, the West Port murderer and also the last public hanging, of murderer George Bryce in 1864.

Below: Corner of the Lawnmarket and George IV Bridge, *c.* 1930. The buildings on the corner of George IV Bridge were demolished in the late 1960s to make way for new council buildings.

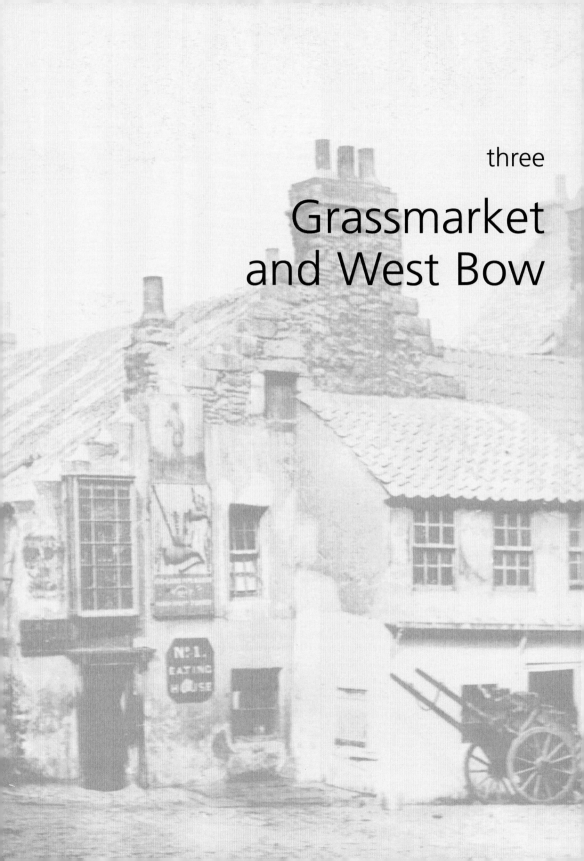

three

Grassmarket
and West Bow

The Grassmarket lies in the valley under the imposing gaze of Edinburgh Castle. An almost enclosed space of 230 yards in length, it was bounded by the West Port, the Cowgatehead, West Bow and Highriggs. The site was being used in the fourteenth century but its importance grew from 1477 when King James III granted a charter for the holding of markets in the area. This included a timber market and a fair for the sale of produce brought into the city from the surrounding area. Weekly markets were held in the Grassmarket from 1477 right up until 1911 and it became a venue for trading everything from horses and cattle to second-hand goods and corn. Originally described as 'Newbygging under the Castle', the land developed a name synonymous with its purpose and became known as the Grassmarket by 1635.

As it was a centre for mercantile activities, the Grassmarket also grew into an area of taverns and lodging houses to cater for the crowds of people attending the fairs. Inns such as the White Hart and the Black Bull opened up in the 1500s feeding off the lucrative market trade. A carrier's quarter grew on the west side of the Grassmarket and with horse fairs and large numbers of out-of-towners, the inns also developed stabling businesses. By the 1700s the inns were being put to good use as coaching quarters and a network of coaches developed that ran from the inns of the Grassmarket to Glasgow, Newcastle and London. It was not until the arrival of the railway that the coaching trade declined.

The West Bow was an incredibly old, twisty road that connected the Grassmarket to the Lawnmarket and it was down this road that condemned prisoners were brought on their way to be hanged. In the early 1830s however most of the ancient buildings were demolished to create a new road called Victoria Street which linked the Grassmarket to the new George IV Bridge. It created a very elegant, sweeping street quite at odds with the seventeenth-century tenements it replaced.

With its fairs and taverns the Grassmarket was always a hive of activity and spectacle; it did however have a darker side as it was the site of the gallows for the hanging of common criminals up until 1784. The site of the gallows is marked by the Covenanter's Monument to commemorate those who were hanged here during a period of religious persecution in the seventeenth century. The Grassmarket assumed an even seedier aspect with the building of the New Town and during the nineteenth century spiralled into squalor becoming an area of extreme poverty. The last century however saw it returning to its mercantile roots as it was reborn as a picturesque tourist and entertainment Mecca with its pubs, hotels and shops.

Opposite above: Edinburgh Castle from the Grassmarket by W.D. Clark, 1858.

Opposite below: Edinburgh Castle from the Grassmarket, *c.*1903. These photographs demonstrate the changes in the Grassmarket during the forty-five years between them. In the earlier photograph the Black Bull is the tallest building in the row but in the later one it is the smallest; the dilapidated buildings to either side having been replaced by Victorian constructions.

North side of the Grassmarket by Edinburgh Photographic Society, *c.* 1900. The White Hart was established in the 1500s and developed into one of the main coaching inns. It was here that the Westport murderers, Burke and Hare, stalked potential victims.

The Black Bull Inn on the north side of the Grassmarket by Francis M. Chrystal, *c.* 1912. As well as offering accommodation and refreshments, the Black Bull also ran a coaching business with its own stabling and coach houses. Local transportation and a coach to Newcastle left from in front of the inn during the eighteenth century.

Above: Horse fair in the Grassmarket, *c.* 1890.

Right: Horse market by George Malcolm, *c.* 1920. The Grassmarket played host to a variety of markets including corn, timber, livestock and horse markets. The horse sales were held in the coaching quarter of the Grassmarket.

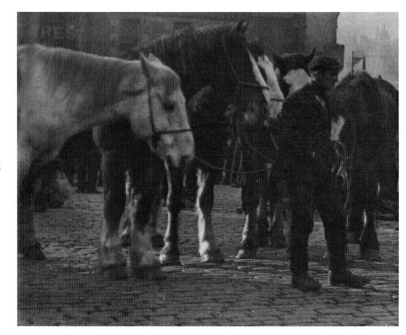

Left: Braun's Close by Francis M. Chrystal, *c.* 1920. Living conditions in the Grassmarket are demonstrated in this view down Braun or Brown's Close. The wall-mounted gas light would have brought welcome light to this narrow, dark close.

Left: Grassmarket Mission, *c.* 1920. In the nineteenth century the Grassmarket developed into an area of slums and extreme poverty. In response hostels and missions for the poor and homeless sprang up including the Grassmarket Mission which opened in 1885. At first the mission offered a ministry to the local population but it developed into a service for the poor and destitute, which it has remained until the present day.

Opposite above: Interior of bric-a-brac shop, West Port by Ron O'Donnell, 1978.

Opposite below: Interior of antique shop in the Grassmarket by Ron O'Donnell, 1978. The inns and hostelries remain part of the local landscape but the twentieth century saw the historical image of the Grassmarket being exploited by a rash of antique and bric-a-brac shops.

Nos 74–82 Grassmarket, *c.* 1900. A group of tenements from different periods, including one with a seventeenth-century door lintel bearing the inscription 'Honour God for all his gifts 1634'.

Old house at the corner of the Vennel and Grassmarket by Francis M. Chrystal, 1907. Here we see the house prior to demolition and reconstruction. Many houses in the Grassmarket at the time were deemed unstable and demolished. They were however rebuilt very closely following the original design so as not to damage the character of the area. This form of sympathetic upgrading was at odds with the destruction of many buildings that occurred in Edinburgh in the 1960s and '70s.

Street ventriloquist in the Grassmarket by Francis M. Chrystal, *c.* 1914. The Grassmarket was always a place of open-air entertainment, with its markets and macabre pastime of watching public hangings. Here however an entranced crowd are intently watching a street ventriloquist.

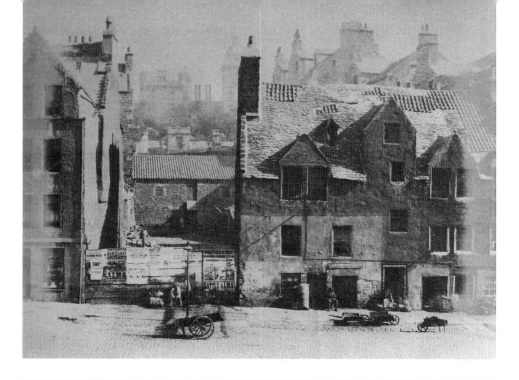

'Quiet afternoon', Grassmarket by A.J. Urquhart, 1956. Here the low walls of the Covenanter's Memorial provide a useful resting spot for this group of men. The memorial marks the place where over 100 men were hanged between 1680–88, for signing the covenant objecting to the introduction of bishops into the Kirk.

Opposite above: South side of the Grassmarket by Dr Thomas Keith, *c.* 1856. These buildings were on the opposite side of the Grassmarket from the coaching inns of the Black Bull and White Hart. The wide space of the Grassmarket has recently been used again for fairs including farmers, craft and antique markets.

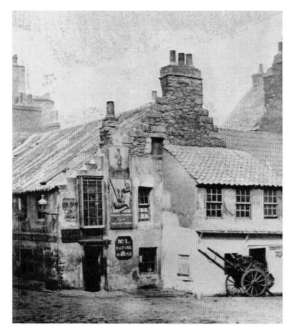

Right: Entrance to the West Port by Thomas Begbie, *c.* 1858. This very early photograph shows the wonderfully named No.1 Eating House and a highland bagpipe maker at the West Port.

Old houses, Main Point, West Port, 1914. Main Point was the name of the customs house built in the 1770s. This image shows a replacement building, the original one had been built for the collection of the two penny custom – a duty on beer that came into force in 1690.

Left: West Port by Bournanville, 1950. As the name suggests the West Port was the western entry into the burgh. The actual gate was demolished in 1786 but the area is still known by this name today. It is infamous for the West Port Murders, the name given to the crimes of Burke and Hare.

Below: 'Sunshine in the Grassmarket' by Richard McIntosh, 1956. A snapshot of street games in the rundown Grassmarket. This photograph was submitted as part of the Edinburgh Public Libraries Photographic Competition in 1956, which has added a rich source of social photographs to the Edinburgh Room's collections.

Right: West Bow by W.D. Clark, 1858. The Bow was an ancient, twisting road that joined the Grassmarket to the Lawnmarket. It had some of the most ancient and quirky buildings in the burgh. The top half was destroyed by the formation of Victoria Street and Terrace.

Below: Dancing in the slums, at the foot of the West Bow by George Malcolm, *c.* 1914. These children are having great fun playing in the cobbled streets of the West Bow. To the right-hand side a lady appears to be playing a large barrel organ so perhaps they were dancing to her musi*c.*

Victoria Street from George IV Bridge, *c.* 1875.

Victoria Street and Terrace by Bournanville, 1950. In the early 1830s Victoria Street cut through the old housing of the West Bow and other closes. It was designed as part of an improvement scheme in conjunction with George IV Bridge to link the bridge to the Grassmarket.

Robert Cresser's brush shop, Victoria Street by James L.A. Evatt, *c.* 1958. Robert Cresser's, a specialised ironmonger shop, was opened in 1873 and operated at several addresses in the city. The shop became a local landmark, looking unchanged from Victorian times but sadly the shop closed this year.

Lamplighter on Victoria Terrace, *c.* 1930. An atmospheric photo of a lamplighter or 'leerie' as they were known, lighting a gas lamp on Victoria Terrace. Gas lighting was still a feature in many parts of Scotland after the introduction of electricity so lamplighters were still a common sight until the 1960s.

'The Arches', Victoria Terrace by
J.R.S. Robson, 1953.

Victoria Terrace by George Malcolm,
c. 1930. Victoria Terrace was a pedestrian
terrace, built above the north side of
Victoria Street. It supports a row of
tenements and has stairs leading up to
the Lawnmarket and down to Victoria
Street. This was home to the Edinburgh
Mechanic's Subscription Library that was
founded in 1825 and was one of the first
libraries aimed at the working man.

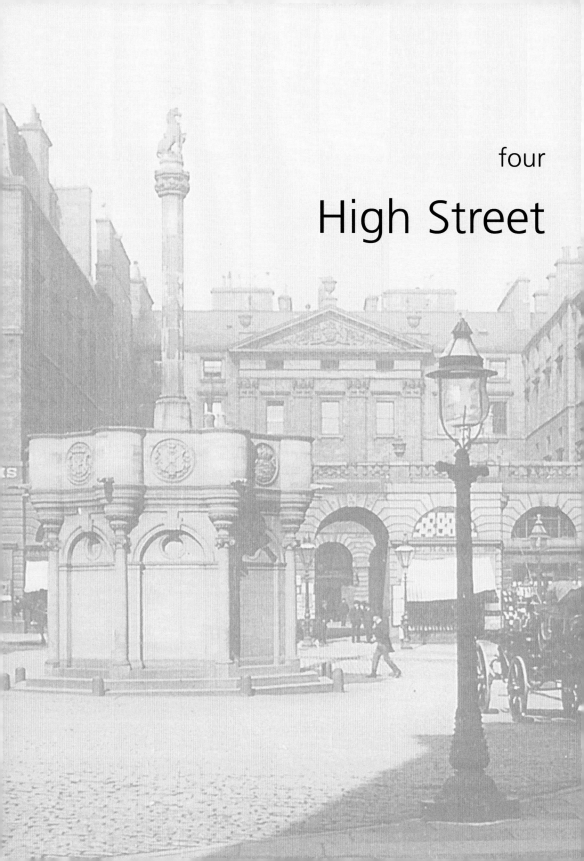

four

High Street

Stretching from the Lawnmarket to the Netherbow Port and Burgh of Canongate, the High Street is the heart of the Old Town in every sense. Destined by geography to be the main road of the burgh, it lies on the ridge of the volcanic tail that leads from Edinburgh Castle down towards Holyrood. By the sixteenth century it was known as the Magnus Vicus, or Great Street, by the next century however it was firmly known as the High Street.

It was not just the name that was 'high' but the buildings too! The constant wars with the English meant the population stayed as close to the castle as possible and this led to the housing climbing ever skyward and the development of the Edinburgh 'land', a tall narrow house. The crowding of the High Street led to severe problems of sanitation. To avoid having to come down from the top of a house, the residents would simply throw household and bodily waste out of the window. This happened every night and was accompanied by the famous cry of 'Gardyloo', which came from the French term *gare l'eau* – 'beware of the water'. The very sensible rhetorical cry was 'haud yer hand!'. In addition each house had dung heaps and pigs lived in the bases of the buildings and roamed the street. Stench and filth filled the High Street and when it rained it washed down the closes into the Nor' Loch which became a stinking swamp.

For all the squalor though the High Street really was the heart of the burgh, being home to St Giles Church, the burgh's Mercat Cross, Parliament House and the City Chambers. The High Street today is also a venue for the Edinburgh Festival and Fringe with street theatre and fairs taking over the road for the month of August.

St Giles Church, *c.* 1847. The original building on the site dates from the twelfth century and has evolved over the years creating a combination of medieval, Gothic and Renaissance styles. The distinctive crown-shaped spire was added in the fifteenth century.

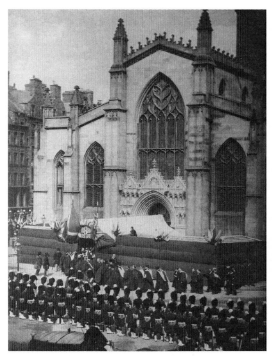

Right: Procession of clergymen attending the reopening of St Giles Church in May 1883. St Giles underwent major remodelling in 1883 and the present interior comes from this time, as does the facing of the outside with stone.

Below: The Heart of Midlothian by John Patrick, *c.* 1900. The heart shape in the cobblestones outside St Giles is known as the Heart of Midlothian. It marks where the entrance to the Tolbooth was before it was demolished in 1817. The Tolbooth as its name suggests was built in 1561 to collect tolls but it went on to become a prison and a place from where criminals were taken to be hanged. Today there is a popular myth that you will bring yourself good luck if you spit in the centre of the heart.

St Giles Church from the West, *c.* 1900. St Giles is often known as St Giles Cathedral even though there are no cathedrals in the Church of Scotland. This is probably a throwback from when it had cathedral status in the seventeenth century. It is more accurately called the High Kirk of Edinburgh.

The High Street, showing the shops in the entrance to the City Chambers, *c.* 1900. The arched colonnades at the front of the City Chambers are now open and lead into the Piazza. Here though we can see them with shops between the arches. When first built it had space for forty shops, plus housing, coffee shops and a customs house.

The City Chambers and a horse-drawn tram by John Wilson, 1957. Construction started on the City Chambers building in 1754, originally however it was called the Royal Exchange. It was designed as a space for the merchants of Edinburgh to gather and conduct business, rather than the open air venue of the Mercat Cross which had been used previously.

Laying the foundation stone for the new part of the City Chambers, 1900. The Town Council gradually took over possession of the building in the nineteenth century as the merchants became reluctant to use the facilities, preferring the local taverns and coffee houses. Extensions were required however to expand the space and these were undertaken between 1898-1903.

Left: A proclamation at the Mercat Cross in Queen Victoria's reign, by George Malcolm, *c.* 1890. The Mercat Cross was a place where the merchants of the burgh would gather to discuss business. It was also used as the place to issue official proclamations and for public executions.

Below: Royal proclamation, February 1952.

The High Street with the City Chambers, 1929. The buildings to the right of the chambers include the entrance to Allan's Close. This close was suppressed during the extension of the City Chambers from 1930-34. There is no longer an entry from the High Street but part of the building remains within the chambers towards Cockburn Street.

Outside stairs, Old Post Office Close by Edinburgh Photographic Society, *c.* 1900. As the name suggests this was once the site of the first post office, in the seventeenth and early eighteenth centuries. At first there was only one postman to cover the whole of the burgh. The close was demolished in 1932 to make way for an extension to the City Chambers.

Gillespie's shop by Edinburgh Photographic Society, 1903.

Advocates Close and old houses on the High Street by Edinburgh Photographic Society, *c.* 1900. The buildings have not changed but the nature of the shops have. Always an area of commerce, the businesses of the High Street used to provide the local residents with basic provisions. Today however most shops here cater to Edinburgh's thriving tourist trade.

'At the well' by George Malcolm, 1958. Here a girl is drinking from the water fountain in front of St Giles Church. The buildings at the back are Parliament House and the Signet and Advocates Libraries. Originally the square was home to a collection of booths and workshops called the Luckenbooths. The shopkeepers had their businesses at ground level and lived in the upper floors.

Cockburn Street by Alexander A. Inglis, *c.* 1897. It is named after Lord Henry Cockburn and was originally called Lord Cockburn Street. He was a judge in Edinburgh from 1834 until his death in 1854.

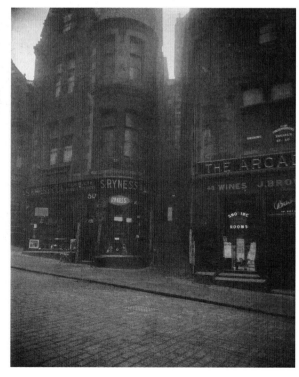

Cockburn Street showing Jackson's Close, *c.* 1900. The narrow Jackson's Close was home to three generations of the Jackson family and hence was named after them.

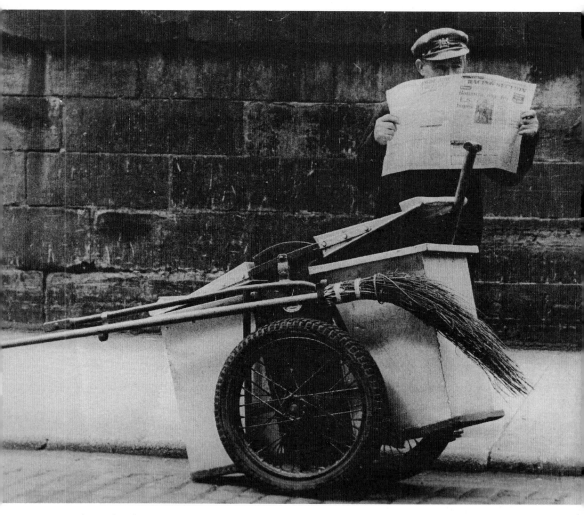

Street Cleaner by the *Evening News, c.* 1950. John Dunbar Henretty was a familiar sight on Cockburn and Market Streets from the 1930s to the 1970s. He was also known as Jock Scaffy Henretty, scaffy being Scots slang for a street cleaner (coming from the word scavenger). Edinburgh is a considerably cleaner place that it used to be: Thomas Carlyle once, poetically, described Edinburgh as a 'stinking, reeky mass of stones and lime and dung'.

Right: The Tron Church by J. & H.S. Storer, 1820. The building of the Tron Church or Kirk was begun in 1636. It is named after the salt-tron, a weighing beam, which was sited outside the church. The area around the church is still known as the Tron today, even though the beam itself was removed in the eighteenth century.

Right: New Tron Kirk Steeple by Thomas H. Shepherd, 1829. The original square tower of the Tron Kirk has been replaced by a slender steeple, after its destruction in the great fire of 1824. The new spire was completed by 1828 and the building continued to be used as a church until 1952.

Opposite above: The City Hotel at No. 69, Cockburn Street, *c.* 1880.

Opposite below: Inglis Wine and Spirit Merchant at No. 69, Cockburn Street by R.K. Thomson, *c.* 1895. These two photographs show the development of a family business from hotel to spirit merchant. The building of Cockburn Street began in 1860 and Alexander Inglis was one of the first proprietors on the street with his City Hotel. Alexander must have died in 1875 as his wife Agnes took over the business in that year and ran the hotel for another twenty years. It is most likely their son Walter Scott Inglis turned No. 69 into a spirit merchants in 1895 but the business was short lived, closing in 1898.

Allan Ramsay's shop in the course of demolition photographed by Edinburgh Photographic Society, 1899. Ramsay occupied this house between 1711–25 and from here sold sheets of his poetry for a penny.

Allan Ramsay's house and shop, *c.* 1864. Allan Ramsay senior was a celebrated Scottish poet, playwright and bookseller. He had this shop in the High Street until 1725 when he moved his business to the Luckenbooths beside St Giles Church. From there he established Scotland's first circulating library and stocked it with 30,000 books. He was condemned by Calvinists for corrupting townsfolk with 'villainous profane and obscene books and playes…lent out, for an easy price'. Edinburgh soon became and has remained a city of libraries which has no doubt contributed to its gaining the UNESCO title of City of Literature.

Right: John Knox House, *c.* 1900. This scene shows the large well outside John Knox House. This was part of a system of wells running the length of the Royal Mile that supplied the Old Town with its only source of water. Water would be carried in buckets from the wells back to the houses.

Below: Moubray House steps, *c.* 1935. Built in 1477 by Robert Moubray, this is the oldest building on the High Street. The house was used by Daniel Defoe to edit the *Edinburgh Courant* in the eighteenth century.

Left: Looking up the High Street from John Knox Corner by George Malcolm, *c.* 1930. Here a fine old gentleman enjoys his pipe beside one of the Old Town's many wellheads. The Tron Kirk can be seen on the left and the crown spire of St Giles Church in the background.

Left: View of the Netherbow Port from the east, 1764. The Netherbow was the entrance into the burgh and where customs were collected. Over the years the building became more elaborate ending with this ornate structure of a two-storey gatehouse and towers. The port was pulled down on the order of the city magistrates in 1764, the year this picture dates from.

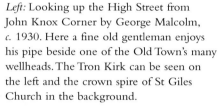

Opposite above: John Knox House and the Canongate, 1856.

Opposite below: John Knox House, *c.* 1900. Despite the name, this building, dating from 1450, has nothing to do with John Knox, the founder of the Church of Scotland. Legend has it that Knox delivered a speech from the bow window of the house although there is no proof that this ever happened. There is little difference in the forty years between these two photographs and the view is still virtually unchanged today.

Custom House, Netherbow by Alexander A. Inglis, 1858. The old Custom House occupied one floor of the tenement to the left during the early part of the eighteenth century. These buildings were demolished in the mid-nineteenth century.

New Palace Cinema, 18-20 High Street by the *Evening News*, 1929. The Art Deco-style New Palace Cinema was opened in 1929 and provided seating for over one thousand cinema goers. It presented both silent and talkie films, opening with *The Great Picture* starring Belle Bennett. Known as a 'flea pit' by locals, the aisles were regularly fumigated during shows much to the discomfort of the audience. The New Palace closed in 1957 and was turned into a food hall.

five

Canongate

The Canongate or Canons Gait (gait being Scots for road) was the name for the road that linked Edinburgh to the Abbey at Holyrood. King David I granted the Augustinian canons the right to have their own burgh between the King's royal burgh and the abbey, resulting in the growth of the Canongate. The street is older than the foundation of the abbey in 1128, as it was always an entrance into the burgh of Edinburgh. Originally the road was called 'Herbergake' which comes from the Saxon word 'herberg' which means an inn. The Canongate was bounded at the top by the High Street and at the bottom by Holyrood and the Watergate.

With the expansion of the palace of Holyroodhouse in the sixteenth century the burgh of Canongate grew enormously in terms of size and status due to the people living there being connected with the royal court. Canongate Tolbooth, built in 1591, was the focal point of the burgh, housing the council chambers, the law court and jail. The coat of arms for the Canongate can be seen on the Tolbooth – a stag's head with a cross between its horns and the words 'This is the way to paradise'. The Canongate ceased to be a separate burgh and merged with Edinburgh in 1856 much to the displeasure of its townsfolk.

Canongate from the top of the gasworks chimney by William Ranken, 1896. The Edinburgh gasworks was located behind the Tolbooth in New Street. Gaslight made an early appearance in Edinburgh life as the company was formed in 1818 by an Act of Parliament. This view also shows the smog which made Edinburgh famous as 'old Reekie'.

Looking down St Mary's Wynd from the junction with the Cowgate by J.G. Tunny, 1854. A horse-drawn furniture cart turns the corner at the top of St Mary's Wynd. The wynd was the original road leading from the south to the Netherbow and was the site of the iron market in Edinburgh.

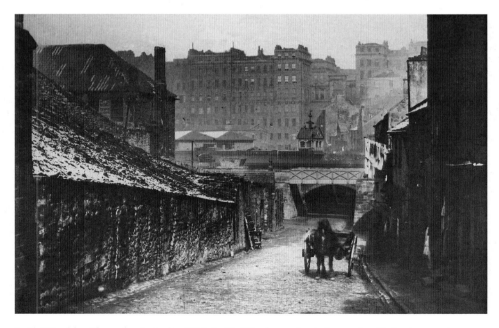

Leith Wynd by Alexander A. Inglis, 1890. Leith Wynd was situated near the Netherbow and originally connected the Canongate with Leith. It was defensive in nature with many of its buildings being fortified. There was also a port, or Watergate, closing off the foot of the wynd, which was connected to a length of the city wall running from the Nor' Loch.

Nisbet of Dirleton's House, *c.* 1900. Located at the top of Reid's Close, this was the house of Sir John Nisbet of Dirleton, a judge and Lord Advocate of Scotland. He is famous for his single-minded pursuit of the covenanters. Built in 1664 it is a crowstep-gabled tenement, the front of which was rebuilt in the original style in 1953.

Morocco Land, *c.* 1880. A carved Moor can be seen on the front of this interestingly named, eighteenth-century tenement. It relates to the tale of Andrew Gray, who fled to Morocco to escape execution and there became the Commander of the Emperor's navy. On his return to Edinburgh in 1645 he dramatically cured the provost's daughter of the plague, married her and then lived in Morocco Land.

The Canongate, *c.* 1900. View of the entrance to St John's Street from the Canongate. It was named after the cross of St John which stood nearby, marking the boundary between the Canongate and Edinburgh. One of the remaining eighteenth-century houses in the street is now the Scottish headquarters for the Order of St John.

The Canongate showing the entrance to Little Jack's Close by A.H. Rushbrook, *c.* 1930. In this close stood the hall of the Corporation of Cordiners (shoemakers) of the Canongate. They would annually elect a cobbler king who would be carried through the burgh in his kingly robes before a coronation celebration was held in the close.

Left: Buckie wife, *c.* 1880. Buckie wives were a common sight on the streets of Edinburgh, with their baskets of cockles, mussels and periwinkles slung across their brows. They would sell little saucers of the seafood topped with vinegar from their regular pitches in the city.

Below: Horse-drawn trap near the Canongate Tolbooth, 1910. Huntly House faces the Tolbooth across the busy Canongate, a main thoroughfare for the horse-drawn traffic of Edinburgh. Huntly House was purchased by the city in 1924 after it was threatened with demolition and turned into a museum.

Right: Moray House by Thomas Begbie, *c.* 1858. Moray House was built in 1628 by Mary, the Dowager Countess of Home. It passed to her daughter Margaret, wife of the 4th Earl of Moray, and remained in the Moray family for several generations. The building still has the original ornate plaster ceilings with heraldic motifs and an impressive entrance flanked by obelisks.

Below: Canongate by Alexander A. Inglis, *c.* 1880. Moray House, on the right, was occupied by Oliver Cromwell during his visits to Edinburgh in 1648 and 1650 and was also used for discussions prior to the Act of Union in 1707. It has also belonged to the British Linen Company, North British Railway Company and the Free Church. Finally in 1846 it became a teacher training college, which it has continued to be up until the present day.

Moray Free Church, 1910. This church was built around 1856 on ground granted from Moray House's garden. Unfortunately this unusually designed church now lies empty and boarded up.

Canongate Tolbooth, c. 1930. The clock was added to the Tolbooth in 1884, shortly after a major restoration in 1879. The building today houses the Peoples Story, a museum that focuses on Edinburgh's social history from the eighteenth century onwards.

Right: Canongate Tolbooth by Archibald Burns, *c.* 1870. The Tolbooth was built in 1591 and was the civic centre of the Canongate Burgh. It contained the jail, council chambers and law courts. Built in the French style it is five-storeys high and remains the oldest building in the Canongate.

Below: Canongate Church by Alexander A. Inglis, *c.* 1880. The original church for the Canongate was the Abbey Church of Holyrood, however, in 1687 this was turned into a chapel for the Order of the Thistle. King James VII and II donated money for the building of a new church for the Canongate which was designed by James Smith in an unusual curved design and completed in 1691. The churchyard contains the original Canongate Mercat Cross and the grave of Agnes McLehose, otherwise known as Clarinda, Robert Burns's love.

Reid's Close by J.L.A. Evatt, 1955. Reid's Court was at No. 95 Canongate and was named after the Reid family that inhabited it, who were smiths and coach makers during the seventeenth and eighteenth centuries.

Above: Buckie wife, Canongate, *c.* 1880. A busy day in the Canongate with a buckie wife selling her wares on the street. Other streetsellers can be seen farther up the street and a little boy in the background is playing with a wheel.

Opposite above: The Canongate, 1922. This view of the Canongate shows the lower half of the north side with the entrance way to Reid's Court marked by stone pillars. Reid's Court probably dates from the 1680s when John Reid, a smith, owned property here. The court has been many things, including a coach yard and a manse. It was the Canongate Manse until 1832 and then following restoration became the manse again in 1958. The pillars are now the only recognisable structure in this picture – all the others have been replaced.

Huntly House by Francis M. Chrystal, 1907. Huntley House was originally three houses, the first of which was built in 1517 and was linked to the others in 1570. The building is known as Huntly House due to the Dowager Duchess of Gordon, a member of the Gordon of Huntly family, renting a flat there in the eighteenth century.

The Watergate, from J. & H.S. Storer's *Views in Edinburgh*, 1820. The Watergate archway stood to the north of Abbey Strand and was the entrance into the Burgh of Canongate. Originally the archway was made of stone and is known to have been there in 1544. It was however blown down in 1822 and replaced by a wooden one that survived barely thirty years.

The Watergate at the foot of the Canongate by Thomas Begbie, *c.* 1858. This part of the Canongate was originally a very upper-class area but with the building of the New Town, and the resulting exodus of the moneyed classes, it turned into an area of poverty.

North side of the Canongate, 1898.

Foot of the Canongate, c. 1930. Within the space of thirty years the gap at the base of the Canongate has been built on using an appropriately sympathetic style. We also see the introduction of a police box, which was once a common sight on Edinburgh streets; most have now been removed or converted into coffee stands. These buildings are directly opposite where the new Scottish Parliament building is sited.

six

Cowgate

The Cowgate is probably the second oldest street in Edinburgh, formed next after the High Street. It is half a mile long and connected the Grassmarket to the South Back of the Canongate at the foot of St Mary's Wynd. Dating at least from the 1300s, its unusual name is probably derived from the Scots 'Coo Gait' or 'Cow Road'. The name refers to the fact that cattle were driven into the city to market or out to pasture by this route.

The Cowgate encompasses the extremes that can be found within the history of the Old Town. In the fifteenth century it was home to the patrician quarter, a street of mansions known as 'Palaces of the Cowgate'. With its wide road, the Cowgate was more suited to the carriages of the nobility than the narrow High Street. Eventually though it descended into poverty and became 'the last word for all that was most hopeless in all Edinburgh'.

Most of the Cowgate has been demolished leaving the Tailor's Hall, built in 1644, as the oldest surviving building. A huge fire broke out in the Cowgate in 2002 tragically leading to the loss of several buildings in this area. The resulting gap is to be redeveloped as a hotel and a group of leisure facilities. The Cowgate is now mostly home to a mixture of bars and the backs of buildings such as the Central Library and Court Houses. The Cowgate, therefore, has not quite regained the glory of its aristocratic past. It will be interesting to see how the redevelopment of the fire site affects the Cowgate environment.

Cowgatehead, Grassmarket and part of Candlemaker Row by J.G. Tunny, 1854. The point where the Cowgate meets the Grassmarket is known as Cowgatehead. This early photograph shows Nos 10-12 Grassmarket, the right-hand side of which later went on to become the Greyfriar's Hotel, one of many hostels for the poor.

Right: Allison's Close, Cowgate, by Francis M. Chrystal, *c.* 1912. After the removal of Hope House its place is taken by the imposing six-storey public library. The buildings to the left of the library have now also been demolished leaving a space for the proposed extension to the Central Library.

Below: Houses in the Cowgate demolished in 1887 for the erection of the public library, by Alexander A. Inglis, 1887. The building beside George IV Bridge was Hope House, the home of Sir Thomas Hope, King's Advocate. His house was decorated with many Latin quotations and two of the original inscribed doorways from Hope House were incorporated into the library building.

Left: Magdalen Chapel, by Edinburgh Photographic Society, 1904. The chapel on the right was built in 1541 and dedicated to St Mary Magdalene. It was founded by a local merchant but later was entrusted to the Corporation of Hammermen, a craft guild. It is unique in having the only surviving pre-reformation stained glass in Scotland.

Below: The west end of the Cowgate by Alexander A. Inglis, Edinburgh Photographic Society, 1902. Elevated view of Cowgatehead and Edinburgh Castle with the impressive tower of the Magdalen Chapel in the foreground. The Cowgate façade and tower of the chapel were added by the Hammermen whose insignia can be found above the doorway.

Right: 'Ices' under the arch of George IV Bridge by George Malcolm, 1924. This lady is selling ice cream from a barrow to a large group of women and children. Ice cream was brought to the masses in Britain in the 1850s although royalty and the aristocracy had enjoyed it previously. Hokey Pokey sellers sold ice cream from barrows in the street, their strange nick-name came from a misinterpretation of their traditional call of *Gelati, ecco, un poco* ('ice cream, here a little'). The beginning of the twentieth century saw the end of these sellers with ice-cream instead being sold mainly from shops.

Below: Looking through the arch of George IV Bridge in the Cowgate towards the Grassmarket, by either J.C.H. Balmain or W.D. Clark, *c.* 1864. Finished in 1834, the relative newness of the George IV Bridge is in stark contrast to the dilapidation of the surrounding buildings.

South side of the Cowgate by Alexander A. Inglis, Edinburgh Photographic Society, *c.* 1870. Sanderson, grocer and spirit merchant, is at No. 199 Cowgate, on the edge of photograph. The adjacent shop appears to be derelict.

Cardinal Beaton's House by Archibald Burns, *c.* 1870. The turreted house on the left belonged to David Beaton, Cardinal Archbishop of St Andrew's. He persecuted Lutheran supporters and was generally hated by all. He was murdered in retaliation for the burning at the stake of George Wishart, the Scottish Reformer in 1546.

Right: Tailor's Hall in the Cowgate by Edinburgh Photographic Society, 1903. Local lads stand beside the hall's impressive archway. The hall was built in 1644 for the Guild of Tailors and was used as a theatre in the eighteenth century. The tablet above the archway is decorated with a large set of shears, the insignia for the corporation.

Below: Tailor's Hall, upper storey added by Provost Kincaid and seen from old garden, *c.* 1900. The barrels in the photograph show that this was when it was used as a brewery. It became Campbell's Brewery in the nineteenth century and was one of fifty breweries in the area, although there are none now. The building lay derelict from 1967 until the 1990s when it was turned into a hotel and pub. The Tailor's Hall is now the oldest surviving building in the Cowgate.

Left: Paddy's Market, the Cowgate by Peter Smeaton Rennie, 1905.

Below: Paddy's Market, Cowgate by Peter Smeaton Rennie, 1905. In Victorian times Edinburgh like other Scottish cities had its 'Paddy's Market' where you could buy anything from a bootlace to a full suit of clothing. The Cowgate at this time was home to many second-hand clothes dealers and this even spilled out on to the street with the Cowgate Port Rag Fair, where both sides of St Mary's Wynd was lined with tables of old clothes.

Right: Bull's Close by Alexander A. Inglis, *c.* 1878. This close was named after a merchant called John Bull who owned property in the close. Closes tended to be named after the people that built them or the most prominent person staying there. Names changed over the years to reflect the most recent inhabitants.

Below: The Old Edinburgh Club meeting at the foot of Blackfriar's Street, 1913. Taken just five years after the foundation of the Old Edinburgh Club, this photograph shows a well-heeled group of ladies and gentlemen. The club was founded to preserve evidence of the Old Town's history and buildings and still exists today with its interest now widened to encompass all of Edinburgh.

Elphinstone Court and House in the Cowgate, now demolished, by Francis M. Chrystal, 1907. Built in 1679 by Sir James Elphinstone, these buildings were demolished shortly after this picture was taken. Francis Chrystal photographed many buildings that were due to be demolished in the great wave of improvement schemes that deprived Edinburgh of many of its ancient buildings.

Cowgate Port stretching up St Mary's Wynd, seen from the foot of the Pleasance, by Thomas Begbie, c. 1858. Every road leading out of the burgh terminated at a port that was a control point for security and tolls. The road continued past the Cowgate Port but it was then in the burgh of Canongate and known as the South Back of the Canongate.

seven

George IV Bridge and Beyond

George IV Bridge spans the Cowgate ravine and its construction provided access to the Old Town from the south. Planned following the 1827 Improvement Act, the bridge was constructed between 1829-34 and smashed its way though the ancient closes of Libberton's Wynd and Old Bank Close. It is named after King George IV who died in 1830 during its construction. It is home to arguably the two most important libraries in Edinburgh – the Central Library and the National Library of Scotland. The Central Library funded by Andrew Carnegie is an ornate Victorian building that faces the Art Deco-style National Library across the expanse of the bridge.

Chambers Street links the South Bridge and George IV Bridge and was developed as part of the 1867 Improvement Act. It was named after Sir William Chambers who was active in promoting the Improvement Scheme. It was built over the eighteenth-century developments of Adam, Argyle and Brown Squares as well as the remaining parts of the even older area known as the Society. It became an elegant street filled with beautiful classical buildings such as the Royal Museum and Heriot Watt University (now the Sheriff Courts).

Candlemaker Row runs from the southern end of George IV Bridge down to Cowgatehead and the Grassmarket. It is a steep ancient road where candle making workshops were congregated in the seventeenth century to reduce the risk of fire spreading amongst the Old Town's wooden buildings. The entrance to Greyfriar's churchyard lies off Candlemaker Row. This is where Greyfriar's Bobby and his master are buried and where hundreds of covenanter's were confined before their trials.

Melbourne Place looking north, 1958. Named after the Prime Minister, William Lamb (Viscount Melbourne) in 1836, the stately arches of Melbourne Place were demolished in 1968 to make way for new council offices. The resulting eyesore is now also scheduled for demolition.

Right: 'Bobbing Charlie' at the County Buildings, Melbourne Place by F.M. Chrystal, *c.* 1912. Bobbing Charlie was a blind beggar whose real name is unknown but he was a familiar sight at the turn of the century on George IV Bridge. His nickname came from his habit of bobbing back and forwards whilst holding out his tin mug.

Below: George IV Bridge, *c.* 1900. The view looking down the east side of George IV Bridge towards Chambers Street with the Sheriff Court House in the middle and St Augustine's Church spire in the distance.

Opposite: Foundations of the National Library of Scotland, *c.* 1938.

Left: Site of the National Library by George Malcolm, 1938. The Sheriff Court Building was demolished in 1938, leaving this space for the building of the National Library of Scotland. It took until 1956 for the National Library to open due to the halt on building during the Second World War.

Below: Sheriff Court House, George IV Bridge, *c.* 1900. Built between 1865-8, the Sheriff Court House was designed by David Bryce. The highly ornamental, Italian-style building cost £44,000 to build and was to survive only seventy years.

Left: The Central Library, George IV Bridge, *c.* 1905. Andrew Carnegie sent a telegram to the opening ceremony of the Central Library saying, 'We trust that this library is to grow in usefulness year after year and prove one of the most potent agencies for the good of the people for all time to come'. One hundred and sixteen years later it is safe to say that the library does indeed continue to grow and change to meet the needs of the people of Edinburgh by developing new services and being responsive to changes in technology and society.

Below: The Central Library by Charles S. Minto, *c.* 1935. Built with £50,000 gifted by Andrew Carnegie, the Central Library opened in 1890. It was designed by George Washington Browne in the French Renaissance style. The design from the front is deceptive as there are four further floors below the level of the bridge. Mr Charles Minto was the city librarian and curator from 1953-70.

Right: The Society, bearing the sign of James Doull, joiner, cabinetmaker and undertaker, by Thomas Begbie, *c.* 1858. Here we can see the extremely run down buildings of the area known as 'the Society'. The name came from the Fellowship and Society of Ale and Beer Brewers of the Burgh of Edinburgh who owned this land in the sixteenth and seventeenth centuries.

Below: The Society, by Dr Thomas Keith, *c.* 1856. The Society land ceased to be owned by the brewers at the end of the seventeenth century and it was redeveloped in 1763 as Brown Square.

Brown Square by Dr Thomas Keith, *c.* 1856. The square took ten years to complete and was finished in 1773. Built before the New Town, this handsome street contained mansions for the upper classes and was deemed 'an extremely elegant improvement' to Edinburgh's housing.

Heriot-Watt College by Alexander Wilson, *c.* 1900. This building was originally built for the Watt Institution and School of Arts in 1873. In 1885 the college joined with George Heriot's Trust and formed Heriot-Watt College which later had university status bestowed on it and is still a major educational facility in Edinburgh. The building is now no longer owned by the university and is part of Edinburgh's judicial courts.

Admit the Bearer

TO THE

Platform at the Industrial Museum, to view the Ceremony of Laying the Foundation-Stone, on the 23d October 1861, by

His Royal Highness the Prince-Consort.

No. 762

An original entry ticket to the laying of the foundation stone of the Museum of Science and Art on the 23 October 1861. The museum was originally known as the Industrial Museum and the foundation stone was laid by Prince Albert, Queen Victoria's consort.

Museum of Science and Art, *c.* 1900. The museum, which is today known as the Royal Museum, was opened in 1866. The architect was Captain Fowkes of the Royal Engineers and he aimed to create a Venetian Renaissance style building that was flooded with light. To achieve this he designed a glass roof which had a system of pipes running over it studded with over 5,000 gas burners so that the building could be used in the evening.

Above: Part of Flodden Wall, demolished for extensions to Royal Scottish Museum, *c.* 1900. Construction began on the Flodden Wall in the fifteenth century as protection from the English. It never completely encircled the city, the east side was never finished. Only small areas of the wall remain today, the largest section being at the Pleasance.

Opposite above: Chambers Street, Edinburgh Photographic Society, 1913. The shops at Society Corner included the Museum Bookshop which is here doing a roaring trade. These buildings were demolished and their place is now taken by an extension to the Royal Museum, built in the 1990s, and now known as the Museum of Scotland.

Opposite below: Chambers Street, Edinburgh Photographic Society, June 1913.

Above: Old Greyfriar's Mission by Edinburgh Photographic Society, 1913. The mission would have been connected with Greyfriar's Church and aimed at providing help for the poor of the area, particularly Potterrow. The walls of the Museum of Science and Art can be seen to the left.

Above: Greyfriars Bobby, *c.* 1910. The statue of Greyfriars Bobby at the top of Candlemaker Row commemorates the Skye terrier who refused to leave his master's grave in Greyfriars churchyard. He spent fourteen years sitting on the grave until his own death in 1872. He only left each day at the sound of the one o'clock gun to be fed by a local coffee shop.

Opposite below: Chambers Street by Edinburgh Photographic Society, June 1913, showing Society Corner on the edge of Chamber's Street looking up towards the New North Free Church. The church was built in 1846 near the site of the town's old lunatic asylum, the Bedlam. The building is now a student-run theatre which has appropriately adopted the name, Bedlam Theatre.

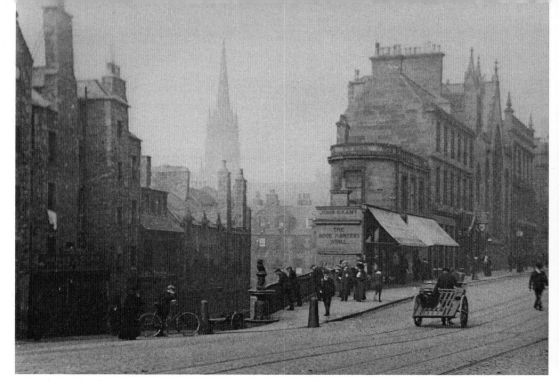

Candlemaker Row from George IV Bridge, *c.* 1910. A view down the steep slope of Candlemaker Row towards the Grassmarket with the spire of the Assembly Hall of the Church of Scotland in the background.

Candlemaker Row by Francis M. Chrystal, *c.* 1912. A view of the buildings at the base of Candlemaker Row prior to demolition.

A tombstone in Greyfriars churchyard, *c.* 1880. The churchyard has an incredible collection of seventeenth-century tombs and monuments. It was also used to imprison 1,200 covenanters before their trial in 1679.

Greyfriars Church by Alexander A. Inglis, *c.* 1900. The site was first inhabited by the Franciscan monastery of Greyfriars and in 1562 Mary Queen of Scots granted land for use as a burial ground. Greyfriars Church was then opened in 1620, taking its name from the monastery. This building was gutted by fire in 1845 leading to the rebuilt church we can see today.

Edinburgh Public Library from Greyfriars churchyard by George Malcolm, *c.* 1925. This view shows the back of the Central Library and its plain brick facing, at odds with the ornate stone decoration on the front entrance from George IV Bridge.

eight
Closes

Looked at from above, the Old Town resembles the bones of a fish, with the castle being the head, Holyrood the tail and the closes the bones coming off the spine. The closes are essentially what the Old Town consists of – rows and rows of narrow lanes bordered by high tenements. The stone tenements were first developed in the early fifteenth century, replacing timber-built buildings and encroaching onto the previously wider streets of the burgh. The need to be near the castle for security was the reason for the tight building pattern and for the height of the housing.

There are some wonderfully named closes such as Old Fishmarket, Sugarhouse and Fleshmarket Close. These were named after businesses that operated from the lane but more often they were named after their builder or a prominent resident, such as Lady Stairs or Baron Maule's Close. Confusingly the names were not a permanent fixture and changed frequently over time as the purpose or main resident of the street altered. Alastair Hardie calculated that there were 497 obsolete names for the closes off the Old Town.

Today there are eighty-three closes, wynds and courts leading off the Royal Mile but this number used to be higher as many streets have been demolished and built over. In the eighteenth century developments such as Mylne's Court and James' Court were created over existing closes in an effort to provide the wealthy with more space than the ancient narrows closes afforded them. The nineteenth century however saw many more closes destroyed as the Old Town burst free from its confines and sprouted bridges such as George IV Bridge, the South Bridge and streets such as Bank Street and Cockburn Street. These all smashed through the existing closes and broad streets were created in their place.

An unidentified close, by Dr Thomas Keith, *c.* 1856. The close may be unknown but this picture captures the essence of what an Edinburgh close was all about – narrow, quirky and run down. The man in the centre of the photograph is posing beside an old cart.

Right: Tenement in Lochend Close by S.G. Jackman, 1950. This tenement stands alone after the demolition of buildings on the north side of the Canongate. It was originally the Highland Society's headquarters which had been formed in the 1820s. They held their first cattle show in 1822 on a piece of ground off the Canongate. The society later became the Highland & Agricultural Society of Scotland and moved to impressive chambers at 3 George IV Bridge.

Below: Little Lochend Close by Peter Smeaton Rennie, 1905. A group of boys shelter in a doorway. This close is distinguished from the other Lochend Close by the word 'little' as this was the narrower of the two.

Left: St John's Close, *c.* 1900. Doorways in the ancient close of St John's. The close was named after the Knights of St John who lived in this area.

Below: St John's Street, *c.* 1900. This grand street was built as part of a scheme for civic improvement beginning in 1768. It has a considerable literary history: it was the home of Tobias Smollett, the novelist, and James Ballantyne, the partner of Sir Walter Scott. Robert Burns also frequently stayed here during his visits to Edinburgh.

Right: Elphinstone House in South Gray's Close, Cowgate by Francis M. Chrystal, 1912. Elphinstone House was a tall tenement built around a paved area. It was constructed in 1679 by Sir James Elphinstone and was inhabited by a succession of aristocrats until the construction of the New Town. South Gray's Close was also home to the Royal Mint of Scotland from 1574–1877 and was in fact called Mint Close at one time.

Below: Campbell's Close by Francis M. Chrystal, 1912. No. 87 Canongate was the home of the gentry and clergy. This close was named after George Campbell, a meal merchant, who owned property here in the seventeenth century.

White Horse Close, 1870. The site was used as the royal mews in the sixteenth century and then was turned into the White Horse Inn around 1623 by Laurence Ord. It is believed that Ord named the inn after Mary Queen of Scots favourite horse. The inn operated as a terminus for coaches travelling to and from Newcastle and London.

Edinburgh City Mission Service in Whitehorse Close, 1914. The Edinburgh City Mission was founded in 1832 by a group of local churchmen. It was a non-denominational organisation that aimed to provide 'practical religion outside the walls of the church'. The city was split into sections, each with its own missionary, so this must have been the Old Town section. The mission still operates within Edinburgh today.

Group of tenants in White Horse Close, May 1912. This large group of women and children were resident in the close and benefited from the recently upgraded accommodation. The site was also renovated in 1965 when a new frontage was built facing the Canongate by Frank Mears, the son-in-law of the great Edinburgh conservationist Patrick Geddes. Geddes had been responsible for the original renovation and its adaptation into working class housing.

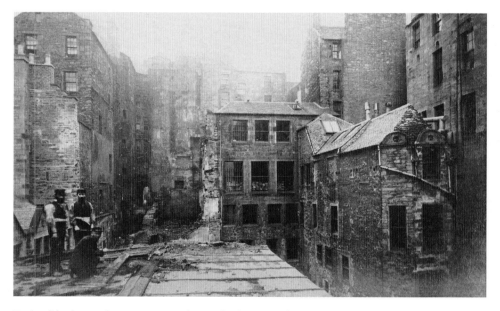

Back of the houses between Byers Close and Advocates Close, by Archibald Burns, c. 1870. The house on the right is said to be the house of Adam Bothwell, Bishop of Orkney. He was Abbot of Holyrood House and ran Holyrood Abbey and estate in the sixteenth century. He was also responsible for marrying Mary Queen of Scots to the Earl of Bothwell and crowning James VI. The house was built around 1630 but as the bishop died in 1593 it is unlikely he knew much about it!

Fishmarket Close by Alexander A. Inglis, *c.* 1870. The Mercat Cross was sited at the head of Fishmarket Close until 1756 and its position is still marked by a circle in the cobblestones.

Left: Fleshmarket Close from Cockburn Street, *c.* 1930. The macabre name relates to the meat market that was sited here on the slope leading down to the slaughterhouse on the edge of the Nor' Loch. In keeping with the theme it was also where the Whigs met at the Bone Marrow Club in Cameron's Tavern.

Opposite: James Court by H.D. Wyllie, *c.* 1930. Children have fun in the snow at James Court, built in 1725 by James Brownhill. Gone are the lime trees that used to grace the garden in the time when David Hume the philosopher had his home here.

Left: Bakehouse Close by Thomas Begbie, 1860. This street was once known as Huntly Close due to Huntly House being at the head of it. The current name however dates from 1832 when the Incorporation of Bakers of the Canongate had a bakehouse in the close.

Below: Bakehouse Close by R.A. Hill, 1968. Here an extension is being built on to the Huntly House Museum in Bakehouse Close. Major renovations were also conducted after 1924 when the council purchased Huntly House to prevent it being demolished. Huntly House is now the Museum of Edinburgh with collections which cover prehistoric to modern times.

Warriston Close looking down to Cockburn
Street, *c.* 1920. Warriston Close was once the
home of John Knox and later named for the
judge, Lord Warriston, who was a leading
covenanter.

Bull's Close, Canongate, *c.* 1920. Bull's Close was
the home of May Drummond, the preaching
quakeress, who inspired the poetry of Alexander
Pope and Joseph Spence. The close was named
after her for a short time but it became Bull's
Close in the early eighteenth century for the
wright, Robert Bull.

Opposite: Advocates Court by Archibald Burns, *c.* 1870. One of the narrowest closes in the Old Town. Not surprisingly this close is named after an advocate – James Stewart, to be precise. He was Lord Advocate of Scotland and lived here from 1619-1713.

Left: Interior view of Milnes Court, *c.* 1912. Milnes or Mylnes Court was the first development of the Lawnmarket that built houses for the gentry round a square rather than the traditional design of narrow streets. It was built in 1690 and it was here that Bonnie Prince Charlie's officers were boarded in 1745.

Below: Milnes Court by George Malcolm, 1934. Children playing in the great playground that was Milnes Court. Always a residential area, the Old Town was home to more than 25,000 men, women and children in 1750.

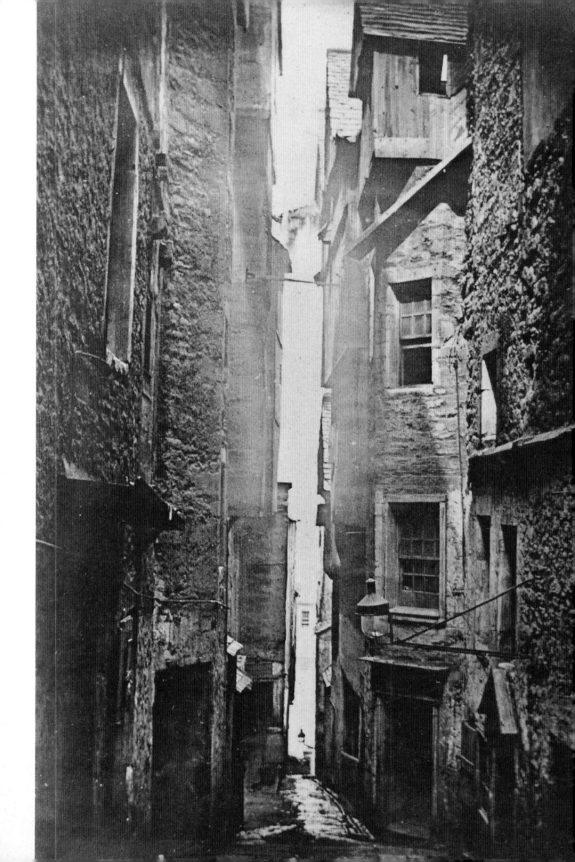

James Court by H.D. Wyllie, *c.* 1930. James Court is situated off the Lawnmarket and originally had five closes leading into it; by 1817 this had reduced to three. Here children are enjoying playing in some rare Edinburgh sunshine.

Chessels Court, Canongate and Excise Office by Francis M. Chrystal, *c.* 1912. The excise office was the scene of the infamous Deacon Brodie's last robbery in 1787. Unfortunately for him his gang only made off with the princely sum of sixteen pounds and one of his accomplices turned King's evidence against him. Brodie fled to Holland only to be captured and returned to Edinburgh to hang for his many crimes.

Right: Riddle's Court by Edinburgh Photographic Society, *c.* 1900. Children posing in their Sunday best within Riddles or Riddel's Court. It was named for George Riddell, a wright and burgess, who built a 'land' here in 1587. The close is famous as being the site of a schoolboy rebellion over holidays in the sixteenth century that resulted in Bailie John McMorran, the city treasurer, being shot dead.

Below: Leith Wynd by Alexander A. Inglis, *c.* 1890. As the name suggests this was part of a road that led to the important shipping port of Leith. Leith was a separate burgh but its fortunes were intertwined with Edinburgh, which provided a market for the goods brought into the port. Leith ceased to be a separate burgh in 1920 and became part of Edinburgh.

Wardrop's Court by George Malcolm, *c.* 1940. Wardrop's Close is unique in having its entrance guarded by four carved dragons. The close was originally home to the Incorporation of Baxters (Baxter being an old name for baker). The close was later named after John Wardrop, a mason who built property here in the eighteenth century.

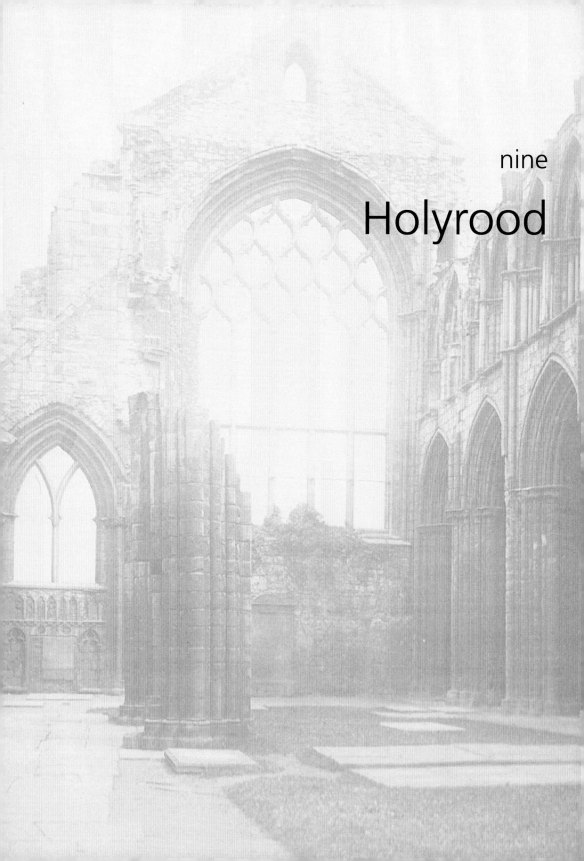

nine

Holyrood

Legend has it that in 1128 King David I went hunting, despite being forbade by his priest, on the feast day of the Holy Rood (*rood* is a Scots word for cross). Whilst hunting in the area that is now Holyrood a huge white stag startled his horse and the king was thrown from his horse. The stag turned to charge upon the fallen king so David prayed to God to save him. Whilst he prayed a cross appeared between the stags antlers and as the beast reached the king, David raised his arms to protect himself and grabbed onto the cross wresting it from between the antlers. Miraculously the stag disappeared before it could harm the King. David then vowed to build a shrine to the Holy Rood on the site where the miracle had happened which led to the foundation of Holyrood Abbey.

Augustinian canons were brought from St Andrew's to the new abbey and it flourished until the Glorious Revolution of 1688 sent it into decline. As the abbey's importance at the site deminished and the palace grew, stone was often taken from the abbey to support building works on the palace. In 1758 the abbey roof was repaired with stone slabs but this led to the collapse of the vault and north side. The abbey soon became a picturesque ruin lying in the shadows of the ever more opulent palace. In the early twentieth century the restoration of the abbey was proposed but it was deemed impossible due to the amount of stonework missing from the building.

The Palace of Holyroodhouse was originally a royal guesthouse for the King to visit the Abbey. It was added to over successive centuries and went on to become the monarchy's official residency in Scotland. In 1503 the guesthouse was extended by James IV and then James V added the royal apartments in 1528-32. The look of the palace changed completely with its reconstruction in 1633 for the coronation of Charles I and then the addition of a new frontage by royal stonemason Robert Mylne for Charles II. Today the palace and abbey are open to the public when the Queen is not in residence.

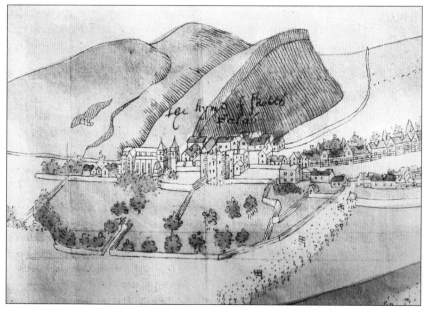

Attack on Edinburgh by English troops under the Earl of Hertford, 1544. The drawing shows Holyroodhouse or 'the Kyng of Scotis Palas' with Arthur's Seat and Salisbury Crags. The attack was part of the 'rough wooing' of Scotland by England. Henry VIII tried to engineer the marriage of his son Edward to the infant Mary Queen of Scots, to prevent the catholic French from gaining control of Scotland. The abbey at Holyrood was severely damaged during this time, and the south of Scotland was ravaged by the Earl of Hertford, until 1548 when the Treaty of Haddington arranged the marriage of Mary to the Dauphin of France.

The gates to Holyroodhouse, 1863. This view of Holyrood shows the James IV tower on the left, built in 1501 for his marriage to Margaret Tudor. This is virtually the only remaining sixteenth-century part of the palace.

Holyroodhouse and Arthur's Seat, c. 1900. There is an enduring myth that Arthur's Seat is named after the Celtic hero King Arthur. However, in all likelihood it comes from a corruption of the Gaelic phrase *Ard-na-said*, meaning height of arrows, which would fit with its role as a defensive position.

Palace of Holyroodhouse from the gardens, 1930. This view of Holyroodhouse is from the north garden and shows the Mary Queen of Scots sundial. It was so named because it was believed to have been created for the Queen but it was in fact made for Charles I. The sundial was designed in 1633 by John Mylne, the master mason, and consists of a polyhedron head carved with heraldic arms including the thistle and rose.

Forecourt of Holyroodhouse, 1870. The 20ft tall fountain in front of Holyrood was built for Queen Victoria but it is a replica of one at Linlithgow Palace, which was built for James V. It is Gothic in design with many heraldic devices, topped with a globe and Scottish lion rampant.

Holyroodhouse Abbey, *c.* 1900. This view of the abbey shows the oracle window, a five-part traceried window that was installed in 1633. That year the abbey underwent restoration as part of the preparations for the coronation visit of Charles I. From this point the emphasis at Holyrood switches from the abbey to the palace and the abbey begins to go into decline.

Interior of Holyroodhouse Abbey, *c.* 1900. Here the destruction that occurred when the nave collapsed in 1768 can be seen. The abbey had been re-roofed in 1758 using slabs of stone. The weight, however, proved too much for the building to withstand and ten years later the vault and lower storeys on the north side collapsed.

Abbey Strand showing the position of the 'Sanctuary Stones' with children awaiting adoption, 1905. The children are standing on the brass setts, marked with the letter S, that show the place where a stream crossed the street and gave it the name. The stones also mark the area of sanctuary offered by the abbey to criminals. Ever since the abbey was founded in 1128 it offered sanctuary (or girth) to all who came within its boundaries. Anyone accused of a crime could ask the church for help and they would administer a pre-trial, conducted by the 'maisters of girth', to determine whether they should be handed over to the state.

Abbey Strand from the east, 1912. The strand marked the boundary between Holyrood Abbey and Canongate Burgh. The word *strand* is the Scots word for rivulet.

Right: Queen Mary's Bath by Edinburgh Photographic Society, 1904. Queen Mary's Bath stands by the northern approach to the palace yard and its purpose has long been the subject of argument. It dates from Mary's restoration of the palace in the sixteenth century. It was believed that there was a bath on the second floor in which Mary Queen of Scots indulgently bathed in wine. It is more likely (if a little less interesting) that the building was a gardener's pavilion. It was restored in 1852 during which a dagger was ominously found hidden in the roof.

Below: Abbey Strand by Edinburgh Photographic Society, 1890. This view of the Strand shows the north side with its sixteenth century tenement blocks. Next to these stand the crow-stepped gabled roof building named after the tavern owner 'Lucky Spence'. This was a seventeenth-century extension to the tenements on its left.

Other local titles published by The History Press

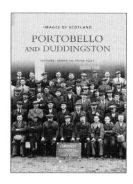

Portobello and Duddingston
MARGARET MUNRO AND ARCHIE FOLEY

This fascinating collection of over 200 images provides a pictorial history of Portobello, famous as a seaside holiday resort, and the adjoining parish of Duddingston, which still maintains its rural village life centred around the church and the loch, despite the advance of suburbia. The result is a volume which will delight anyone who has lived in, worked in or even visited Portobello or Duddingston.

0 7524 3657 0

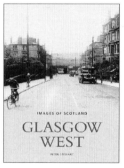

Glasgow West
PETER STEWART

This fascinating collection of more than 220 archive images, many never published, explores the history of the west of Glasgow over the last 150 years. Much has changed over that time, but many of the area's Victorian and Edwardian terraces retained their grandeur as fashions and faces evolved around them. This nostalgic volume will delight anyone who has lived or worked in the west of Glasgow and provides a valuable social record of the way things were in this thriving city.

0 7524 3658 9

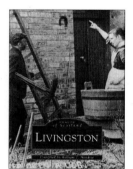

Livingston
WILLIAM F. HENDRIE

Livingston is West Lothian's largest town. During the past forty years over 40,000 people have chosen to call it home. Before the 1960s few beyond the immediate area had even heard of it. That changed in 1962 when a new town was needed to relocate people from overcrowded Glasgow. Livingston's classification as one of Scotland's official new towns resulted in dramatic growth and is now the administrative, economic and shopping centre for the whole of West Lothian.

0 7524 1888 2

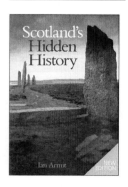

Scotland's Hidden History
IAN ARMIT

People have lived in Scotland for at least 10,000 years. Yet, for the first 9000 of these years, no recognisable concept of 'Scotland' even existed. Most books on Scottish history dispose of these nine millennia in a brief introduction, before moving on to the more familiar kings, queens, barons and battles of medieval Scotland. Ian Armit tells the story of Scotland's earliest history by concentrating on 100 of the most exciting and accessible monuments.

0 7524 3764 X

If you are interested in purchasing other books published by The History Press, or in case you have difficulty finding any of our books in your local bookshop, you can also place orders directly through our website
www.thehistorypress.co.uk